Fast K·1
F··d

KÖNEMANN

Fast kids' food

This book is aimed at children aged 6 and up, but don't let the kids have all the fun, the whole family can enjoy these recipes.

❖ ❖ ❖

Pleasing children is difficult, especially when they seem to prefer everything that is bad for them. Food affects the way children grow, so it is important to give them a balanced diet. This doesn't mean that every meal has to be balanced, just that over each day the foods should add up to a balance. If fruit and vegetables are missing at lunch, make up for it in the afternoon with a snack of vegetable crudites or fruit pieces.

Young children should never be put on a diet, unless you have been advised to do so by a doctor. All the food groups are essential for growth and development. However, a childhood spent eating junk food is not healthy and will contain far too much fat. Food cooked by you will be far more nutritious and healthy.

Children won't automatically like a new food—don't be disheartened, but try again a few days later. Remember that things that are hated one day can be firm favourites by the following week.

Sweet foods should not be used as rewards or bribes, as this gives them added value in your child's mind.

Children tend to know how much to eat. They eat when they're hungry and until they are full, without having to be forced. Children's appetites also fluctuate, depending on whether they are going through a period of slow or rapid growth. Overweight children tend to be that way because they are offered too much food. Give small servings and allow for second helpings, so no-one is daunted by the food.

Snacks must be instant and accessible, as well as healthy, otherwise it is easier to open a packet of crisps or biscuits. Try to make fruit always available. Some ideas are nuts, dried fruit, carrot and cucumber sticks, yoghurts, fresh fruit jellies and icy poles made with fruit juice.

Drinks can be high in sugar. Water, fresh juices, fruit milkshakes, whips and cordials are much better than carbonated soft drinks. Add soda water to fruit juices for a healthier fizzy drink and freeze ice-cube trays of orange and lemon juice to add to drinks.

Meat and poultry are often served up to children as fillets and pieces rather than meat on the bone. However, children often like cutlets and chops, chicken drumsticks and wings. Ready-cooked barbecue chickens are useful for sandwiches, tortillas, enchiladas, bakes, pasta dishes and home-made pizzas. Kebabs are fun, but take them off the skewers before giving to very young children.

Fish is often seen as tricky to cook, but this need not be the case. Choose very fresh firm-fleshed white fish that does not have bones (ask your fishmonger). Fish and chips does not have to be a greasy meal—fish fillets can be dipped in flour then lightly fried and served with baked potato wedges, tomato ketchup or tartare sauce. Children often enjoy seafood, especially prawns and calamari rings.

Carbohydrates should form the biggest part of most meals. Potatoes are an excellent source of carbohydrates and can be cooked in many different ways. A boring boiled potato can be transformed into delicious mash in a matter of seconds and may well be more acceptable in this form. A good repertoire of mash recipes can be useful—mix with green veggies for bubble and squeak, with sweet potato or pumpkin for a change of colour, or serve with lots of gravy.

Vegetables are often the most hated foodstuff of children and the hardest to make sure they eat. If they prefer vegetables raw, then don't bother trying to cook them. It can be easier to persuade children to eat carrot sticks while watching TV than to eat cooked vegetables with their dinner.

Dairy products are important for children's calcium intake, as well as providing a good source of protein. Children's calcium requirements are high and the Australian Nutrition Foundation recommends 3 serves of high calcium foods (ie dairy products such as milk or cheese) a day. If you are using soy milk, make sure it has added calcium.

Pulses and grains can be a great way of getting protein into your child's diet if he or she is not a great meat-eater. They are a good source of fibre.

The final ingredient for a healthy child is plenty of exercise. About 20–30 minutes three or four times a week is recommended, but the more the better. Exercise is more enjoyable as a family affair, and that way everyone will benefit!

This book is designed for adults cooking for children, but most of the recipes are easy and many can be attempted by older children on their own. Younger children may enjoy helping with the preparation.

Fast kids' food

The serving sizes in this book are reasonably sized and are suitable for adults or older children. Halve if you have younger kids.

Banana apricot muesli muffins

*Ready to eat in
30 minutes
Makes 12 muffins*

1¼ *cups (155 g) plain
flour*
1¼ *teaspoons
bicarbonate of soda*
³/4 *cup (90 g) untoasted
muesli*
¹/2 *cup (35 g) All-bran
cereal*
³/4 *cup (90 g) sultanas*
¹/4 *cup (45 g) chopped
dried apricots*
³/4 *cup (185 g) sugar*
¹/4 *cup (60 ml)
vegetable oil*
¹/2 *cup (125 ml) milk*
*1 ripe banana,
mashed*
1 egg
³/4 *cup (185 ml)
buttermilk*

Crumble Top
¹/2 *cup (60 g) plain
flour*
*2 tablespoons brown
sugar*
1 teaspoon cinnamon
60 g butter

1. Preheat the oven to moderately hot 200°C (400°F/Gas 6). Sift the flour and bicarbonate of soda into a large bowl, then add all the other dry ingredients. Combine the oil, milk, banana, egg and buttermilk, add to the mixture and fold gently until just combined.
2. For the crumble top, combine the flour, sugar and cinnamon in a bowl. Rub in the butter until it resembles coarse breadcrumbs.
3. Grease or line 12 x ¹/2-cup (125 ml) muffin holes and fill to three-quarters full with the mixture. Sprinkle on the crumble top and cook for 20 minutes, or until a skewer inserted into the middle comes out clean. Remove from the tin and cool on a wire rack.

NUTRITION PER MUFFIN
*Protein 2.5 g; Fat 5.5 g;
Carbohydrate 24 g; Dietary
Fibre 1.5 g; Cholesterol
15 mg; 648 kJ (155 cal)*

Banana apricot muesli muffins

Hawaiian French toast

*Ready to eat in
  15 minutes
Serves 6–8*

*225 g can crushed
  pineapple
4 eggs
1 teaspoon vanilla
  essence
1 tablespoon maple
  syrup
1 tablespoon caster
  sugar
/ cup (60 ml) milk
200 g tub plain yoghurt
8 slices day-old bread
80 g butter*

1. Drain the pineapple and place in a food processor or blender with the eggs, vanilla, maple syrup, sugar, milk and a tablespoon of the yoghurt. Process until smooth, then transfer to a shallow bowl or dish.
2. Trim the crusts from the bread and halve each slice diagonally. Soak a few at a time in the pineapple batter until it's well absorbed on both sides but not too soggy.
3. Heat half the butter in a large frying pan until foaming. Fry the bread in batches over medium heat until browned on both sides, adding the remaining butter as needed.
Keep each batch warm as you make the next batch. Serve warm with the remaining yoghurt.

NUTRITION PER SERVE (8)
*Protein 15 g; Fat 23 g;
Carbohydrate 47 g; Dietary
Fibre 2.5 g; Cholesterol
230 mg; 1892 kJ (450 cal)*

Note: Honey may be substituted for maple syrup if you prefer.

Breakfast apple pancakes

*Ready to eat in
  30 minutes
Serves 4*

*30 g butter
1 egg
1¼ cups (315 ml) milk
¼ cup (60 g) caster
  sugar
½ teaspoon vanilla
  essence
1½ cups (185 g) self-
  raising flour
2 green apples, peeled,
  cored and grated
butter, for cooking
maple syrup, to serve*

1. Melt the butter in a pan or microwave on High for 10–15 seconds. Transfer to a jug and add the egg, milk, sugar and vanilla. Whisk together well.
2. Sift the flour into a bowl, then gradually whisk in the liquid ingredients until you have a smooth batter. Stir in the apple. Pour the mixture back into the jug for easy pouring.
3. Heat 1 teaspoon of butter in a large frying pan until it is foaming, then add ¼ cup of the mixture for each pancake (depending on your frying pan, you should be able to cook 2–3 at a time). Spread out a little with the back of a spoon and cook for 2 minutes, or until bubbles appear on the surface. Flip the pancakes over and cook for a further minute on the other side until golden. Stack the pancakes on a plate covered with a tea towel and keep warm.
4. Cook the remaining batter, adding more butter to the pan for each batch as you need it. Serve hot with the maple syrup.

NUTRITION PER PANCAKE
*Protein 3 g; Fat 5 g;
Carbohydrate 20 g; Dietary
Fibre 1 g; Cholesterol
30 mg; 555 kJ (130 cal)*

Note: Different fruit can be used, such as dried bananas, fresh blueberries and chopped strawberries.

*Hawaiian French toast (top) and
Breakfast apple pancakes*

7

Chicken stix

*Ready to eat in
30 minutes
Serves 4–6*

*2 cloves garlic, crushed
2 teaspoons grated
fresh ginger
1/2 cup (125 ml)
teriyaki sauce
1 tablespoon honey
1 teaspoon sesame oil
500 g chicken
tenderloins, halved
lengthways
3 cups (90 g) cornflakes
3 tablespoons sesame
seeds*

1. Preheat the oven to moderately hot 200°C (400°F/Gas 6). Combine the garlic, ginger, teriyaki sauce, honey and sesame oil in a large bowl. Add the chicken, toss to coat, then cover and refrigerate until needed.
2. Place the cornflakes in a large plastic bag and crush roughly with your hands (you could get your kids to help out with this). Add the sesame seeds.
3. Drain the chicken, discarding any extra marinade, and place in the bag with the cornflakes. Shake well to make sure the chicken is well coated.
4. Place the chicken on a well-greased baking tray. If any of the coating comes off the chicken, press it back on. Cook for about 10–12 minutes, or until the chicken is cooked through and golden brown. There is no need to turn the pieces over during cooking.
5. Serve hot with a mayonnaise or sweet chilli dipping sauce.

NUTRITION PER SERVE (6)
*Protein 20 g; Fat 5 g;
Carbohydrate 17 g; Dietary
Fibre 1 g; Cholesterol
40 mg; 840 kJ (200 cal)*

Baked ham, egg and cheese rolls

*Ready to eat in
20 minutes
Serves 4*

*4 round bread rolls
90 g shredded ham
1 1/2 cups (185 g) grated
Cheddar
4 eggs*

1. Preheat the oven to moderately hot 200°C (400°F/Gas 6). Cut a slice from the top of the rolls and hollow out the bread, leaving a 1 cm wall. Place the bread shells on a baking tray.
2. Divide the ham and 1 cup of the cheese between the rolls, then break a whole egg into the top of each one. Bake for 5 minutes, then remove from the oven and sprinkle with the extra cheese. Return to the oven and bake for 5–7 minutes, depending on how you like your egg cooked.

NUTRITION PER SERVE
*Protein 30 g; Fat 25 g;
Carbohydrate 45 g; Dietary
Fibre 3 g; Cholesterol
230 mg; 2145 kJ (512 cal)*

Note: Process the leftover bread in a food processor and freeze in a plastic bag for breadcrumbs.

*Chicken stix (top) with
Baked ham, egg and cheese rolls*

Mini beef kebabs

Ready to eat in
20 minutes
Makes 12 skewers

12 mini bamboo
  skewers, about 15 cm
  long (see Note)
225 g can pineapple
  pieces, drained
3 zucchini, thickly
  sliced into 24 pieces
250 g rump steak, cut
  into 2 cm cubes
24 cherry tomatoes
1/4 cup (60 ml)
  barbecue sauce

1. Place the skewers in
a bowl of cold water to
soak. This will stop
them burning while the
kebabs are cooking.
Drain, then thread a
piece of pineapple, a
slice of zucchini, a cube
of steak and a cherry
tomato onto each
skewer. Repeat so that
you have two sets of
ingredients per skewer.
Brush with some of the
barbecue sauce.
2. Heat a large, non-
stick frying pan and
cook the skewers for
5–10 minutes, or
until cooked through,
turning once and
basting with the
remaining barbecue
sauce. Serve with some
steamed rice.

Mini beef kebabs (top) with
Spinach and ricotta frittata

NUTRITION PER SKEWER
Protein 5.5 g; Fat 0.5 g;
Carbohydrate 5 g; Dietary
Fibre 1 g; Cholesterol
15 mg; 200 kJ (48 cal)

Note: If not available,
cut longer skewers
down to size using
kitchen scissors. If you
have more time, soak
the skewers for up to
30 minutes.

Spinach and ricotta frittata

Ready to eat in
30 minutes
Serves 4

250 g orange sweet
  potato, cut into
  1 cm cubes
2 teaspoons oil
1 clove garlic, crushed
1/2 small red onion,
  sliced into thin wedges
150 g English spinach,
  trimmed and shredded
60 g ricotta
3 eggs, lightly beaten
1/4 cup (30 g) grated
  Cheddar

1. Place the sweet
potato in a large pan of
salted water and bring
to the boil. Cook for
10 minutes, or until
just tender. Drain well.
2. Meanwhile, heat the
oil in a 20-cm non-stick
frying pan. Add the
garlic and onion and

stir over medium heat
until the onion begins
to soften. Add the
spinach and toss until
the spinach has wilted.
Stir through the cooked
sweet potato and
remove from the heat.
3. Whisk the ricotta
until smooth and
gradually add the eggs
(the mixture may look
slightly lumpy). Season
with salt and freshly
ground black pepper.
Pour the mixture over
the vegetables in the
pan and stir gently,
then swirl the pan to
distribute the egg
mixture evenly. Sprinkle
the cheese over the top.
Preheat the grill.
4. Return the pan to
the heat and cook over
a low-medium heat for
5–8 minutes, or until
the eggs are almost
cooked through. Place
under the grill for
3–5 minutes, or until
the top is set and the
cheese melted. Slide the
frittata out of the pan
and onto a plate,
cheese-side-up, and cut
into wedges. It can be
served hot or cold.

NUTRITION PER SERVE
Protein 10 g; Fat 10 g;
Carbohydrate 10 g; Dietary
Fibre 2.5 g; Cholesterol
150 mg; 745 kJ (180 cal)

Note: A wedge of
cold frittata is great
for lunch boxes.

Avocado and tomato salsa with corn chips

Ready to eat in
15 minutes
Serves 4

2 ripe avocados,
    halved
2 ripe tomatoes, finely
    diced
2 spring onions, finely
    chopped
1 Lebanese cucumber,
    finely diced
1 tablespoon olive oil
2 teaspoons white wine
    vinegar
100 g corn chips

1. Peel the avocados
and remove the stone.
Dice the flesh and
gently toss together in a
large bowl with the
tomato, spring onion,
cucumber, olive oil and
white wine vinegar.
2. Serve the salsa piled
high in serving bowls,
surrounded by the
corn chips.

NUTRITION PER SERVE
Protein 5 g; Fat 35 g;
Carbohydrate 15 g; Dietary
Fibre 5.5 g; Cholesterol
0 mg; 1780 kJ (430 cal)

Note: You can also use
this salsa as a delicious
filling for warm soft
flour tortillas or lavash
bread, or put in a
small tub for your
child's lunch box.

Chicken kebabs with colourful salsa

Ready to eat in
20 minutes
Serves 4

8 bamboo skewers
4 chicken breast fillets,
    cut into bite-size
    cubes
1/2 cup (125 ml)
    barbecue marinade
1 loaf Turkish bread,
    halved lengthways
    through the centre
lettuce leaves, to serve

Colourful Salsa
2 large tomatoes ,finely
    chopped
1 Lebanese cucumber,
    finely chopped
1 peach or nectarine,
    stoned and finely
    chopped
1/2 cup (25 g) chopped
    fresh coriander or
    parsley

1. Place the skewers in
a bowl of cold water to
soak. This will stop
them burning while the
kebabs are cooking.
Preheat a grill or
barbecue hot plate.
2. Thread the chicken
cubes onto the skewers
and place in a shallow
dish. Coat with the
barbecue marinade,
cover and refrigerate
until ready to use.
3. To make the
colourful salsa,
combine the tomato,
cucumber, peach and
coriander in a bowl.
4. Cut the Turkish
bread into 8 slices, then
grill the cut surfaces.
5. Remove the skewers
from the marinade
(reserving the
marinade) and place
in a single layer, well
spaced out, on the hot
grill or barbecue hot
plate. Cook for
3 minutes, then turn
and cook for a further
3 minutes until cooked
through. Brush with the
reserved marinade
during cooking.
6. Remove the skewers
and arrange the chicken
and lettuce leaves on
the Turkish bread.
Serve with the salsa.

NUTRITION PER SERVE
Protein 30 g; Fat 3 g;
Carbohydrate 30 g; Dietary
Fibre 3 g; Cholesterol
55 mg; 1130 kJ (270 cal)

Note: You could use
mango or paw paw
instead of the peach.
Sprinkle the salsa with
balsamic vinegar or
lemon juice for a more
tangy taste. Left-overs
will make a delicious
sandwich the next day.

Avocado and tomato salsa with corn chips (top)
and Chicken kebabs with colourful salsa

Chicken burgers

*Ready to eat in
20 minutes
Serves 4*

350 g chicken mince
4 spring onions, finely
  chopped
3/4 cup (75 g) dried
  breadcrumbs
1 egg
1 tablespoon oil
4 rolls
2 tablespoons
  cranberry sauce
1/2 cup (30 g) alfalfa
  sprouts

1. Using your hands, combine the chicken mince, spring onions, breadcrumbs and egg in a large bowl. Shape into 8 hamburger patties, no thicker than 1.5 cm.
2. Heat the oil in a non-stick frying pan. (Alternatively, use a chargrill pan, grill or barbecue and lightly brush the burgers with the oil before cooking.) Cook the burgers over medium heat for 4–5 minutes each side, or until they are cooked through.
3. Split the rolls in half lengthways and top each base with 2 chicken burgers, 2 teaspoons of the cranberry sauce and some alfalfa sprouts. Replace the top of the roll.

NUTRITION PER SERVE
*Protein 8 g; Fat 15 g;
Carbohydrate 18 g; Dietary
Fibre 1.5 g; Cholesterol
45 mg; 1345 kJ (305 cal)*

Note: Alternative burger toppings include mayonnaise and shredded lettuce, or just tomato sauce.

Tuna and bean tacos

*Ready to eat in
15 minutes
Serves 6*

12 taco shells
2 x 185 g cans tuna,
  drained
1/2 cup (125 g) sour
  cream
1/2 small red onion,
  finely chopped
300 g can cannellini
  or butter beans,
  rinsed and drained
2 cups (90 g) shredded
  lettuce
3 tomatoes, finely
  sliced

1. Preheat the oven to moderate 180°C (350°F/Gas 4) and warm the taco shells for 5–10 minutes while preparing the filling.
2. Break the tuna into chunks and combine with the sour cream, red onion and the beans. Season with salt and freshly ground black pepper.
3. Place some of the lettuce and a couple of slices of tomato in each taco, then fill with the tuna and bean mixture. Serve immediately, allowing two tacos per person.

NUTRITION PER SERVE
*Protein 20 g; Fat 15 g;
Carbohydrate 8 g; Dietary
Fibre 4.5 g; Cholesterol
60 mg; 1306 kJ (297 cal)*

Note: The filling for the tacos also makes a good lunch box salad. Put it in an airtight container and serve the tacos or corn chips on the side.

*Chicken burgers (top) with
Tuna and bean tacos*

LUNCH BOXES

It is important that children have a healthy and nutritious lunch every day that they actually enjoy eating. A balanced lunch should include carbohydrates such as bread, pasta, rice and potatoes; proteins such as meat, fish, cheese and eggs; and fresh fruit and vegetables. Drinks can be yoghurt or milk drinks, fruit juices or water. Junk food and fizzy drinks won't add much nutritious value to a lunch box and are best left out.

Sandwiches can be made from any type of sliced bread, roll, English muffin or rollable bread such as Lebanese breads or pitta pockets. There are lots of delicious sandwich fillings, but avoid things that will make the bread go soggy or are bland and boring. Including relatively wet fillings such as mashed avocado or banana, hummus, cottage cheese, ricotta or chutneys and pickles means that you don't need to use butter or margarine. Rolled breads can be wrapped

in foil to keep their shape, and sandwiches can be wrapped in baking paper or sealed in snaplock bags. An airtight lunch box will keep everything fresh.

Baked foods such as quiches, frittatas and tartlets are good for lunch boxes, as are savoury muffins and scones. Wrap everything separately in foil or plastic wrap to prevent it becoming soggy. Sweet muffins, giant cookies, health bars and slices are good treats and are better than chocolate bars. Salads packed in separate boxes and served with bread make

a change from sandwiches. Try vegetable sticks, fruit pieces or dried fruit served with a dip of hummus or cottage cheese. Or maybe a pasta, rice or potato salad with chicken, tuna or meat. Other salads that work well in a lunch box include tabbouleh, coleslaw and mixed-bean salad.

Drinks in tetrapaks such as fruit juices, yoghurt and milk drinks can be frozen and then put straight in the lunch box. This means they will still be cold when lunchtime comes around and will help keep everything else cool as well.

You can also make your own fruit juices, smoothies and shakes, but make sure you leave enough room for the liquid to expand if you are freezing drinks in your own containers.

It is important that lunch boxes are kept clean and free from bacteria. Empty out any uneaten food and wash the box out daily, then dry it thoroughly before storing, leaving the lid off. If it's a hot day and your child does not have a fridge available for storage at school, add a frozen drink or ice pack to make sure everything stays chilled until lunchtime. Choose a box that is manageable for your child but has enough room to hold everything. Make sure it has a tight seal around its lid, but if your child is very young, check they can remove the lid without any trouble. This also applies to any packing materials inside—little fingers find foil and snaplock bags much easier to handle than plastic wrap.

Lunchbox recipes from left to right: a Banana apricot muesli muffin (page 4); Spinach and ricotta frittata (page 11); an Iced banana smoothie (page 62); Tuna and bean tacos (page 21); Fruche and fruit salad (page 58); Gado Gado (page 30); and a Strawberry soy thickshake (page 62)

Rice with beef strips

Ready to eat in 30 minutes
Serves 4

1 tablespoon oil
1 small onion, chopped
100 g mushrooms, chopped
1 clove garlic, crushed
1 cup (200 g) long-grain white rice
1 1/2 cups (375 ml) chicken stock
400 g rump steak, finely sliced
1 tomato, diced
2 tablespoons chopped fresh parsley

1. Heat the oil in a pan, add the onion, mushrooms and garlic and cook over medium heat for 2–3 minutes, or until the onion has softened. Stir through the rice, then pour over the chicken stock and stir to combine. Bring to the boil, then reduce the heat to low and simmer, covered, for 10 minutes. Leaving the pan covered, remove it from the heat and allow to stand for 5 minutes.
2. Meanwhile, heat a wok or heavy-based frying pan and cook the slices of rump steak on both sides until cooked through. Cut into thin strips. Cover, set aside and keep warm.
3. Add the tomato and parsley to the rice and stir the beef strips through. Season well before serving.

NUTRITION PER SERVE
Protein 30 g; Fat 8 g; Carbohydrate 40 g; Dietary Fibre 3 g; Cholesterol 65 mg; 1495 kJ (355 cal)

Pork with rice stick noodles

Ready to eat in 30 minutes
Serves 4

150 g thin rice stick noodles
2 tablespoons oil
200 g pork eye fillet, thinly sliced
3 cloves garlic, crushed
1 carrot, cut into matchsticks
50 g snow peas, cut lengthways into matchsticks
1 tablespoon soy sauce
1 tablespoon lime juice
2 teaspoons soft brown sugar
1 teaspoon fish sauce
1 tablespoon chopped fresh chives
1 tablespoon chopped fresh mint

1. Soak the rice sticks in boiling water for 5–10 minutes, or until they are soft. Drain and set aside on a clean tea towel to dry.
2. Meanwhile, heat 1 tablespoon of the oil in a wok or heavy-based frying pan. When the oil is hot, fry the pork slices and garlic, in batches, until the pork is cooked through and browned. (Add more oil if necessary.) Remove, set aside and keep warm.
3. Heat the remaining oil in the wok or frying pan and stir-fry the carrot and snow peas for 2–3 minutes over a high heat. Return the pork slices to the wok along with the noodles and toss everything together.
4. Add the soy sauce, lime juice, brown sugar and fish sauce. Toss together until well combined.
5. Just before serving, add the chopped chives and mint and mix together well.

NUTRITION PER SERVE
Protein 15 g; Fat 10 g; Carbohydrate 15 g; Dietary Fibre 2 g; Cholesterol 30 mg; 935 kJ (225 cal)

Note: You can also use fresh rice noodles or rice vermicelli for this dish.

Rice with beef strips (top) and Pork with rice stick noodles

Nachos

*Ready to eat in
  30 minutes
Serves 4*

2 teaspoons oil
250 g beef mince
300 g can red kidney
  beans
200 g jar taco sauce
230 g packet corn chips
1 cup (125 g) grated
  Cheddar
2 tomatoes, chopped
2 spring onions, finely
  sliced
1/2 avocado
1 tablespoon lemon
  juice

1. Preheat the oven to moderate 180°C (350°F/Gas 4). Heat the oil in a frying pan and add the mince. Cook for 5 minutes, or until the beef has browned and most of the liquid has evaporated, breaking up any lumps with a fork. Add the beans and taco sauce and cook, stirring, for another 10 minutes.
2. Divide the mince mixture between four ovenproof plates or shallow soup bowls, keeping the mixture in the centre. Arrange the corn chips around the edge, tucking them slightly into the beef mixture. Sprinkle the cheese over the beef and a little way onto the corn chips. Bake for 5 minutes, or until the cheese melts.
3. Combine the tomato and spring onion and place in the centre of the nachos. Mash the avocado with the lemon juice and place a spoonful on top of each dish.

NUTRITION PER SERVE
*Protein 30 g; Fat 27 g;
Carbohydrate 25 g; Dietary
Fibre 10 g; Cholesterol
70 mg; 1954 kJ (467 cal)*

Caramelized chicken wings

*Ready to eat in
  30 minutes
Serves 4*

1 kg chicken wings
2 teaspoons peanut oil
2 cloves garlic,
  crushed
1 teaspoon finely
  grated fresh ginger
1/4 cup (90 g) honey
2 tablespoons soy
  sauce

1. Cut the tip off each chicken wing and discard. Cut the wings in half at the joint.
2. Heat the oil in a wok or large heavy-based frying pan. Add the garlic and ginger and cook, stirring, over medium-high heat for 1 minute. Add the chicken and stir-fry for 2 minutes until brown.
3. Stir in the honey and soy and cook, covered, over medium heat for 10 minutes. Remove the lid and cook, stirring occasionally, for a further 10 minutes, or until the chicken is tender and caramelized. Serve as a snack or with some steamed rice.

NUTRITION PER SERVE
*Protein 1 g; Fat 12 g;
Carbohydrate 20 g; Dietary
Fibre 0 g; Cholesterol
0 mg; 990 kJ (225 cal)*

*Nachos (top) with
Caramelized chicken wings*

San choy bau

*Ready to eat in
  30 minutes
Serves 4*

8 small iceberg lettuce
  leaves
1 tablespoon oil
2 cloves garlic, crushed
1 stem lemon grass,
  white part only, finely
  chopped
500 g lean pork mince
1 carrot, finely chopped
2 spring onions, finely
  chopped
60 g water chestnuts,
  finely chopped
1 tablespoon lime juice
1 tablespoon soy sauce
2 teaspoons soft brown
  sugar
2 tablespoons chopped
  fresh coriander
Hoisin sauce, to serve

1. Rinse the lettuce
leaves and gently pat
dry. Set aside on a
serving plate.
2. Heat the oil in a wok
or frying pan. Add the
garlic, lemon grass and
pork mince. Stir-fry
over a high heat for
5 minutes, or until the
mince has browned
and cooked through,
breaking up any lumps
with a fork.
3. Add the carrot,
spring onions and
water chestnuts and
toss until well
combined and heated
through. Add the lime

juice, soy sauce, brown
sugar and coriander
and stir in. Spoon
into the lettuce leaves
and serve with some
Hoisin sauce.

NUTRITION PER SERVE
*Protein 30 g; Fat 7.5 g;
Carbohydrate 6 g; Dietary
Fibre 2 g; Cholesterol
60 mg; 885 kJ (210 cal)*

Note: Chicken mince
can be substituted
for the pork mince.

Baked sesame chicken on toast

*Ready to eat in
  30 minutes
Serves 4*

250 g chicken mince
1 clove garlic, crushed
1 teaspoon grated fresh
  ginger
1 tablespoon oyster
  sauce
2 teaspoons soy sauce
1 teaspoon sesame oil
1 tablespoon chopped
  fresh coriander
1 tablespoon cornflour
8 slices bread, crusts
  removed
1/4 cup (40 g) sesame ·
  seeds
sweet chilli sauce or soy
  sauce, to serve

1. Preheat the oven to
moderately hot 200°C

(400°F/Gas 6). Mix
together the chicken
mince, garlic, ginger,
oyster and soy sauce,
oil, coriander and
cornflour in a bowl.
2. Spread about
2 heaped teaspoons of
the mixture evenly onto
each piece of bread,
right up to the edges.
3. Spread the sesame
seeds out on a plate.
Dip each piece of
bread, mixture-side-
down, into the sesame
seeds. Place on a
baking tray and bake
for 15–20 minutes, or
until the mixture is
golden and cooked
through.
4. Slice each piece in
half and serve with the
sweet chilli sauce or
soy sauce.

NUTRITION PER SERVE
*Protein 20 g; Fat 10 g;
Carbohydrate 30 g; Dietary
Fibre 2.5 g; Cholesterol
30 mg; 1220 kJ (290 cal)*

Note: You can make
these sesame toasts
ahead of time and
freeze them before
baking. Layer in a
container with freezer
wrap between each
layer and freeze for up
to 2 months. When
you want to eat them,
defrost, then bake
as above.

*San choy bau (top) with
Baked sesame chicken on toast*

Noodle pancakes with satay chicken

Ready to eat in
25 minutes
Serves 4

1 packet of 2-minute
  chicken noodles with
  the flavour sachet
2 tablespoons chopped
  fresh chives
1/2 cup (125 ml) oil
1 onion, sliced
250 g chicken
  tenderloins or thigh
  fillets, sliced into
  bite-size pieces
3/4 cup (185 ml) bottled
  satay sauce
1 tablespoon chopped
  peanuts
2 teaspoons chopped
  fresh coriander

1. Pour boiling water over the noodles, allow them to soften, then drain well.
2. Place the noodles in a bowl with the flavour sachet and chives. Mix well and divide into four batches.
3. Heat the oil in a frying pan and fry each batch, flattening the noodles out to form a pancake shape. Turn the pancake over and repeat on the other side. Fry until they are golden and crispy, then drain and keep warm.
4. Strain off any remaining oil in the pan, leaving just 1 tablespoon. Fry the onion for 2 minutes, then add the chicken pieces and fry until browned. Add the satay sauce and peanuts to the pan and simmer, stirring, for 5–10 minutes, or until the chicken is cooked.
5. To serve, place the noodle pancake on a plate, spoon the chicken satay over the top and sprinkle with the coriander.

NUTRITION PER SERVE
Protein 18 g; Fat 45 g;
Carbohydrate 15 g; Dietary
Fibre 2 g; Cholesterol
50 mg; 2405 kJ (445 cal)

Mexican burgers

Ready to eat in
30 minutes
Serves 4

1 small onion
450 g beef mince
1/2 cup (40 g) fresh
  breadcrumbs
1/4 cup (60 ml) milk
1 tablespoon taco
  seasoning mix
2 tablespoons finely
  chopped fresh
  coriander or
  flat-leaf parsley
plain flour, for coating
1 tablespoon butter
2 tablespoons vegetable
  oil
4 hamburger buns
4 lettuce leaves, torn
  into pieces
200 g jar taco salsa

1. Finely grate the onion and put in a large bowl with the beef mince, breadcrumbs, milk, taco seasoning mix and the coriander or parsley. Season with salt and freshly ground black pepper and mix well to combine.
2. Divide the mixture into four and form each portion into a round and flattened burger shape. Lightly coat with the flour.
3. Heat the butter and oil in a large frying pan and add the burgers. Cook over medium heat for 8 minutes each side, or until cooked through.
4. Slice the buns and place the lettuce on the bases. When the burgers are cooked, place them on top of the lettuce and spoon some taco salsa over the top. Top with the other half of the bun and serve with corn on the cob.

NUTRITION PER SERVE
Protein 35 g; Fat 30 g;
Carbohydrate 60 g; Dietary
Fibre 5 g; Cholesterol
85 mg; 2670 kJ (640 cal)

Noodle pancakes with satay chicken (top) and
Mexican burgers

Tuna and potato patties

*Ready to eat in
  30 minutes
Makes 8*

600 g potatoes, peeled
  and cubed
3 spring onions, finely
  chopped
130 g can corn kernels,
  drained
185 g can tuna, drained
  and mashed
2 tablespoons
  mayonnaise
1 egg, lightly beaten
dry breadcrumbs, for
  coating
vegetable oil, for frying

1. Bring a large pan of
salted water to the boil
and cook the potatoes
for 8 minutes, or until
tender. Drain well
and mash, then leave
to cool a little.
2. Put the mashed
potato, spring onions,
corn kernels, tuna and
mayonnaise in a large
bowl and mix together
well. Divide the
mixture into eight
balls and flatten into
thick patties.
3. Place the egg in a
shallow dish and the
breadcrumbs on a
plate. Dip each patty
into the egg, then coat
with the breadcrumbs,
shaking off the excess.
4. Put 1 cm oil in a
large frying pan. Heat

the oil over medium
heat until a cube of
bread browns in
15 seconds. Add the
patties, in batches if
necessary, and cook for
3 minutes, then turn
and cook for a further
3 minutes, or until
golden and cooked
through. Drain the
patties thoroughly on
paper towels and
serve with some
green vegetables.

NUTRITION PER PATTY
*Protein 10 g; Fat 10 g;
Carbohydrate 20 g; Dietary
Fibre 2 g; Cholesterol
35 mg; 860 kJ (205 cal)*

Zucchini frittata

*Ready to eat in
  25 minutes
Serves 4–6*

2 zucchini
1 carrot, finely grated
1 onion, finely chopped
3 bacon rashers, diced
2 teaspoons mixed
  dried herbs
6 eggs
1/2 cup (125 ml) milk
1/2 cup (125 ml) cream
1 tablespoon oil
1/2 cup (60 g) grated
  Cheddar

1. Grate the zucchini
into a colander and use
your hands to squeeze
out any excess liquid.

Add the zucchini to the
carrot, onion, bacon
and dried herbs and
combine well.
2. Mix together the
eggs, milk, cream and
some salt and freshly
ground black pepper.
Pour into the grated
vegetables and
combine well.
3. Place the oil in an
ovenproof non-stick
frying pan, about
28–30 cm in diameter,
and heat the oil over
medium heat. When
hot, add the mixture,
turn down the heat to
very low and cook for
about 10–15 minutes,
or until the mixture is
almost set in the centre
and the sides and
bottom of the frittata
have a nice golden
crust. Preheat the grill.
4. Place the frittata
under the hot grill for
3 minutes, then
sprinkle over the
Cheddar and grill until
melted and golden.
5. Slide the frittata
out onto a serving
plate and slice into
wedges. Serve with a
green salad or some
steamed vegetables.

NUTRITION PER SERVE (6)
*Protein 15 g; Fat 20 g;
Carbohydrate 4.5 g; Dietary
Fibre 1.5 g; Cholesterol
230 mg; 1140 kJ (275 cal)*

*Tuna and potato patties (top)
with Zucchini frittata*

Veal schnitzel with ham, tomato and cheese

Ready to eat in
15 minutes
Serves 4

60 g butter
4 pieces crumbed veal
 schnitzel
4 slices ham
3 tomatoes, sliced
1 cup (125 g) grated
 Cheddar

1. Preheat the grill to medium-hot.
2. Melt half the butter in a large frying pan and fry two of the schnitzels for about 3–4 minutes on each side. Transfer to a baking tray and position under the grill just so they stay warm. Fry the last two schnitzels in the remaining butter, then put them on the tray with the others.
3. Top each schnitzel with a slice of ham. Arrange the tomato slices in a single layer over the ham, dividing them among the schnitzels, then season with freshly ground black pepper. Sprinkle the Cheddar over the top of the tomato.

4. Turn the grill to high and place the plate directly under the heat. Grill until the cheese melts and turns golden. Serve with some steamed vegetables

NUTRITION PER SERVE
Protein 30 g; Fat 40 g;
Carbohydrate 1.5 g; Dietary
Fibre 1 g; Cholesterol
115 mg; 1369 kJ (310 cal)

Salami and tomato pasta

Ready to eat in
20 minutes
Serves 4

325 g penne pasta
$1^1/2$ cups (375 g)
 tomato pasta sauce
4 Roma tomatoes,
 roughly chopped
1 large cabanossi stick
 (about 180 g), sliced
$^1/2$ cup (30 g) chopped
 fresh parsley

1. Bring a large pan of salted water to the boil. Cook the pasta according to the manufacturer's instructions. Drain and divide among four serving bowls.
2. Meanwhile, place the pasta sauce and 1 cup (250 ml) of water in a pan. Bring to the boil and cook for 5 minutes, or until the mixture is slightly thickened. Stir in the tomatoes and cook for a further 2 minutes just to warm the tomatoes through. Add the cabanossi and parsley and heat through. Pour over the pasta, dividing the mixture among the bowls, and serve hot.

NUTRITION PER SERVE
Protein 20 g; Fat 20 g;
Carbohydrate 70 g; Dietary
Fibre 7 g; Cholesterol
50 mg; 2210 kJ (530 cal)

Note: You can use any variety of mild salami instead of the cabanossi. Different types of pasta shapes can be used in this recipe for variety, or try using one of the coloured pastas for a change.

Veal schnitzel with ham, tomato and cheese (top)
with Salami and tomato pasta

Gado Gado

*Ready to eat in
  30 minutes*
Serves 4–6

Peanut sauce
1 tablespoon oil
1 onion, finely chopped
1 clove garlic
*1/2 cup (125 g) crunchy
  peanut butter*
2 teaspoons soy sauce
*140 ml can coconut
  milk*
*1 tablespoon chopped
  fresh coriander*

Accompaniments
baked potato wedges
*1 celery stick, cut into
  batons*
*1 carrot, cut into
  batons*
*4 button mushrooms,
  sliced*
*4 cherry tomatoes,
  halved*
*150 g cauliflower
  florets, lightly
  steamed or
  microwaved until
  just tender*
*150 g broccoli florets,
  lightly steamed or
  microwaved until
  just tender*
*or your own choice of
  vegetables, raw or
  cooked*

1. To make the peanut
sauce, place the oil,
onion, garlic, peanut
butter, soy sauce and
coconut milk in a
blender with 1/2 cup

(125 ml) water and
blend until mixed. Pour
into a pan and bring
to the boil. Reduce the
heat and simmer for
5 minutes, then add the
coriander. Place the
sauce in a bowl.
2. Place the vegetables
on a large platter with
the sauce in the centre
for dipping. Your kids
can dip the vegetables
straight into the sauce.

NUTRITION PER SERVE (6)
*Protein 9 g; Fat 20 g;
Carbohydrate 8.5 g; Dietary
Fibre 5.5 g; Cholesterol
0 mg; 990 kJ (235 cal)*

Couscous with honeyed chicken

*Ready to eat in
  30 minutes*
Serves 4

*1 1/3 cups (245 g)
  couscous*
40 g butter
*1/2 cup (75 g) frozen
  corn kernels*
*1/2 cup (80 g) frozen
  peas*
50 g oil or butter
*500 g chicken
  tenderloins, trimmed
  and cut into bite-size
  strips*
1 tablespoon honey
*1 tablespoon lemon
  juice*
*2 tablespoons chopped
  fresh parsley, optional*

1. Place the couscous in
a bowl and pour in
1 1/3 cups (350 ml)
boiling water. Add
the butter. Leave for
4 minutes while you
cook the corn and peas.
2. Bring a small pan
of salted water to the
boil and add the corn
and peas. Cook for
2 minutes, then
drain well.
3. Fork the couscous
until light and fluffy
and fold through the
corn and peas. Keep
warm while you cook
the chicken.
4. Heat the oil or butter
in a heavy-based frying
pan or wok and, when
it begins to foam, add
the chicken in batches.
Cook for 5 minutes,
stirring, until the
chicken is golden and
cooked through. Stir
through the honey and
lemon juice and scrape
up any brown bits in
the pan. Add a little
water if the mixture
appears too dry.
5. Divide the couscous
among 4 serving plates,
pile the honeyed
chicken on top and
scatter with the parsley.

NUTRITION PER SERVE
*Protein 35 g; Fat 40 g;
Carbohydrate 15 g; Dietary
Fibre 3 g; Cholesterol
55 mg; 2210 kJ (502 cal)*

*Gado Gado (top) and
Couscous with honeyed chicken*

Hokkien noodle and beef stir-fry

*Ready to eat in
20 minutes
Serves 4*

2 tablespoons oil
200 g beef strips
3 cloves garlic, crushed
1 teaspoon grated
  fresh ginger
300 g frozen Thai-style
  stir-fry mixed
  vegetables, thawed
1/3 cup (80 ml) Hoisin
  sauce
250 g Hokkien
  noodles, separated

1. Heat a wok or
heavy-based frying pan
until very hot, add
1 tablespoon of the oil
and swirl it around to
coat the side of the pan.
Add the beef strips and
stir-fry for 2–3 minutes,
or until just browned
and cooked through.
Remove and set aside.
2. Heat another
tablespoon of oil in the
wok and add the garlic
and ginger. Stir-fry for
30 seconds, then add
the Thai-style vegetables
and stir-fry for 2–3
minutes, or until the
vegetables are tender.
Return the meat to the
wok, add the Hoisin
sauce and Hokkien
noodles and toss well

to combine. Cook for a
further 5 minutes, then
serve immediately.

NUTRITION PER SERVE
*Protein 20 g; Fat 15 g;
Carbohydrate 55 g; Dietary
Fibre 8.5 g; Cholesterol
45 mg; 1800 kJ (430 cal)*

Sweet and sour chicken stir-fry

*Ready to eat in
30 minutes
Serves 4*

2 tablespoons oil
300 g chicken breast
  fillet, cut into small
  cubes
1 small onion, chopped
1 red capsicum, cut
  into cubes
2 small carrots, sliced
100 g snow peas, halved
225 g can pineapple
  pieces, drained
1/2 cup (125 g) bottled
  sweet and sour sauce

1. Heat a wok or
heavy-based frying pan
until very hot, then add
half the oil and swirl it
around to coat the side
of the pan. Add the
chicken in batches and
stir-fry until golden
brown and cooked
through. Remove and
set aside.
2. Heat another
tablespoon of the oil in

the wok, add the onion,
capsicum, carrot, snow
peas and pineapple and
stir-fry for 2 minutes,
or until the onion has
softened slightly.
3. Return the chicken
to the wok, add the
sweet and sour sauce
and toss to coat well
and heat through. Serve
with steamed rice.

NUTRITION PER SERVE
*Protein 20 g; Fat 10 g;
Carbohydrate 25 g; Dietary
Fibre 3.5 g; Cholesterol
40 mg; 1195 kJ (285 cal)*

Note: You can reduce
the amount of fat used
in these recipes by
using an oil spray, or by
brushing the wok with
a very thin layer of oil.

*Hokkien noodle and beef stir-fry (top) with
Sweet and sour chicken stir-fry*

Vegetable and potato cakes

*Ready to eat in
30 minutes
Makes 10 patties*

*200 g butternut
pumpkin, peeled and
cut into small pieces
500 g potatoes, peeled
and cut into small
pieces
50 g broccoli, broken
into small pieces
1 1/2 cups (200 g) frozen
diced vegetables
1/2 cup (60 g) grated
Cheddar
1/2 cup (50 g) dry
breadcrumbs
2 tablespoons oil*

1. Steam the pumpkin
and potato for
5 minutes until tender.
2. Meanwhile, bring a
pan of water to the boil
and cook the broccoli
and frozen vegetables
for 2–3 minutes, or
until just cooked. Drain
and place in a bowl.
3. Mash the potato and
pumpkin until smooth.
Add to the vegetables
with the Cheddar and
stir to combine.
4. Place the
breadcrumbs on a
plate. Take a 1/3 cup
of the mixture and
coat all over with the
breadcrumbs, gently
shaping the mixture
into thick round patties
as you coat them.

Repeat with the
remaining mixture.
5. Place the oil in a
large frying pan over
moderate heat. Cook
the patties, in two
batches, over medium-
high heat until they are
golden brown on both
sides. Drain on paper
towels. Serve with a
mixed salad.

NUTRITION PER PATTY
*Protein 4.5 g; Fat 8 g;
Carbohydrate 10 g; Dietary
Fibre 2.5 g; Cholesterol
6 mg; 590 kJ (140 cal)*

Mini meat pies

*Ready to eat in
30 minutes
Makes 6*

*1 tablespoon oil
1 onion, chopped
2 cloves garlic, crushed
250 g lean beef mince
425 g can crushed
tomatoes
220 g can baked beans
1 tablespoon tomato
paste
3 sheets ready-rolled
puff pastry, thawed
2/3 cup (85 g) grated
Cheddar*

1. Preheat the oven to
very hot 240°C (475°F/
Gas 9) and put a
baking tray on the top
shelf. Heat the oil in a
frying pan, add the
onion and garlic and
cook until soft. Add the
beef mince and brown,
breaking up any lumps
with the back of a fork.
2. Add the tomatoes,
baked beans and
tomato paste. Boil for
3–5 minutes, stirring,
until the mixture
thickens slightly.
3. Meanwhile, lightly
grease 6 x 1-cup
(250 ml) muffin holes.
4. Using a 14 cm saucer
as a guide, cut 6 circles
from the pastry sheets.
Cut a small 'V' starting
from the centre of each
circle to the edge, about
2 cm wide at the edge.
Overlap the cut out
section to fit the pastry
into each tin, and press
the join together firmly.
5. Spoon the mixture
into the pastry and
divide the Cheddar
between the pies. Place
on the baking tray in
the oven and bake on
the top shelf for
15–20 minutes, or until
golden and the pastry
is cooked.

NUTRITION PER SERVE
*Protein 20 g; Fat 30 g;
Carbohydrate 30 g; Dietary
Fibre 4 g; Cholesterol
65 mg; 2005 kJ (480 cal)*

Note: This is a great
meal to prepare ahead
and freeze.

*Vegetable and potato cakes (top) with
Mini meat pies*

American sandwich

Ready to eat in
20 minutes
Serves 4

1 tablespoon oil
4 eggs
12 thick slices bread
2 tablespoons
  mayonnaise
2 cups (90 g) shredded
  lettuce
125 g shredded ham
3 Roma tomatoes,
  sliced

1. Heat the oil in a frying pan. Add the eggs and fry for 2–3 minutes, or until the white is cooked and the yolk is still runny.
2. Meanwhile, toast the bread, then spread one side with mayonnaise. Place a slice of toast on four plates. Divide the lettuce among the toast.
3. Place another slice of toast on top. Arrange the ham, tomato and egg on top of this piece of toast. Top with the final piece of toast, mayonnaise-side-down. Serve the sandwich cut into triangles.

NUTRITION PER SERVE
Protein 20 g; Fat 15 g;
Carbohydrate 45 g; Dietary
Fibre 3.5 g; Cholesterol
200 mg; 1665 kJ (395 cal)

American sandwich (top) with
Sloppy Joes

Note: The ham can be substituted with barbecued chicken. Whole-egg mayonnaise has more flavour and less sugar than other types. Home-made mayonnaise should not be given to young children because it contains raw eggs.

Sloppy Joes

Ready to eat in
25 minutes
Serves 4

1 tablespoon oil
1 onion, chopped
400 g beef mince
1 tablespoon plain
  flour
1 cup (250 ml) beef
  stock
1/2 cup (125 g) tomato
  sauce
2 teaspoons
  Worcestershire
  sauce
4 hamburger buns
tomato slices,
  to serve
shredded lettuce,
  to serve

1. Heat the oil in a frying pan and cook the onion for 3 minutes, or until soft. Add the mince and cook for 5 minutes, or until the beef has browned, breaking up any lumps with a fork.
2. Sprinkle the flour over the beef, and cook, stirring, for 1 minute. Slowly pour in the stock, stirring to combine. Add the tomato sauce and Worcestershire sauce and mix well. Bring to the boil, reduce the heat to low, and simmer for 10 minutes.
3. Cut the hamburger buns in half and toast. Lay both halves on four plates and ladle the beef mixture over. Serve with the tomato slices and shredded lettuce on the side.

NUTRITION PER SERVE
Protein 30 g; Fat 18 g;
Carbohydrate 60 g; Dietary
Fibre 4 g; Cholesterol
65 mg; 2210 kJ (530 cal)

Fish kebabs

*Ready to eat in
 25 minutes
Serves 4*

*8 bamboo skewers
1/2 cup (125 ml) lemon
 juice
1 tablespoon chopped
 fresh parsley
1 tablespoon chopped
 fresh coriander
1 clove garlic, crushed
300 g firm white
 fish fillet, cut into
 3 cm cubes
200 g salmon fillet, cut
 into 3 cm cubes*

Corn salsa
*270 g can corn kernels,
 drained
1 large avocado, diced
1 tomato, diced
1 small red onion,
 finely chopped*

1. Soak the skewers in
a shallow dish of water
while preparing the
basting sauce.
2. Combine the lemon
juice, parsley, coriander
and garlic in a bowl.
Divide in half and set
aside. Thread the fish
onto the skewers,
alternating the white
fish and the salmon.
You should have about
3 pieces of white fish
and 2 pieces of salmon
on each skewer.
3. Heat a lightly
greased large frying
pan until hot. Cook

the fish skewers for
3–5 minutes, or until
cooked through,
turning frequently. Use
half the lemon mixture
to brush over the
kebabs as they cook.
4. To make the corn
salsa, place all the
ingredients in a bowl.
Pour over the remaining
lemon mixture and toss
gently to combine.
5. Place 2 skewers on
each plate and serve
with the salsa and
some steamed rice.

NUTRITION PER SERVE
*Protein 30 g; Fat 10 g;
Carbohydrate 15 g; Dietary
Fibre 3.5 g; Cholesterol
75 mg; 1240 kJ (295 cal)*

Salmon cakes

*Ready to eat in
 30 minutes
Makes 10 cakes*

*600 g floury potatoes,
 peeled and cubed
415 g can salmon,
 bones removed,
 drained and mashed
1 small onion, finely
 chopped
1 egg, lightly beaten
1/2 cup (60 g) grated
 cheese
2 tablespoons chopped
 fresh parsley
1/2 cup (50 g) dry
 breadcrumbs
oil, for frying*

1. Place the potato
pieces in a large pan of
salted water and bring
to the boil. Cook for
about 5 minutes, or
until the potato is
tender. Drain well
and mash.
2. Place the mashed
potato in a large bowl,
add the mashed
salmon, onion, egg,
cheese and parsley. Stir
well to combine.
3. Place the
breadcrumbs on a
large plate. Spoon a
generous 1/3 cup of the
salmon mixture onto
the breadcrumbs.
Shape into a round
and coat well with the
breadcrumbs, then
flatten slightly. Repeat
with the remaining
mixture.
4. Heat 1 cm oil in a
large frying pan. Place
the salmon cakes in the
pan, in batches if
necessary, and cook
over medium heat for
2–3 minutes on each
side, or until golden
brown. Drain well on
paper towels and
serve immediately
with some mixed
salad leaves.

NUTRITION PER CAKE
*Protein 15 g; Fat 10 g;
Carbohydrate 10 g; Dietary
Fibre 1.5 g; Cholesterol
55 mg; 845 kJ (200 cal)*

*Fisk kebabs (top) with
Salmon cakes*

Two-minute noodle and vegetable omelette

Ready to eat in 25 minutes
Serves 4–6

2 x 85 g packets chicken or tomato flavoured instant noodles
300 g frozen mixed vegetables
5 eggs, lightly beaten
1/3 cup (80 ml) milk
3/4 cup (90 g) grated Cheddar
2 tablespoons chopped fresh parsley
1 tablespoon oil

1. Bring a large pan of water to the boil and add the noodles with the flavour sachet. Stir to combine, then boil for 2 minutes, drain and set aside.
2. Bring another pan of water to the boil, add the frozen vegetables and cook for 1–2 minutes, or until heated through. Drain well.
3. In large bowl, combine the vegetables, noodles, eggs, milk, cheese and parsley and season with salt and pepper. Toss gently using two forks.
4. Preheat the grill. Heat the oil in a 20 cm ovenproof non-stick frying pan. Pour the noodle mixture into the pan, using a fork to spread the noodles and vegetables out evenly.
5. Cook over medium heat for 3–5 minutes, or until the eggs have almost set. Place under a grill for 3–5 minutes, or until the top has set and is slightly golden. Cool slightly, then cut into wedges and serve with a salad.

NUTRITION PER SERVE (6) *Protein 10 g; Fat 20 g; Carbohydrate 5 g; Dietary Fibre 3 g; Cholesterol 165 mg; 835 kJ (200 cal)*

Cheesy chicken macaroni

Ready to eat in 20 minutes
Serves 6

2 cups (310 g) macaroni
1/2 cup (80 g) frozen peas
1 1/2 cups (375 g) ricotta cheese
1/2 cup (50 g) grated Parmesan
2 tablespoons extra virgin olive oil
1/2 barbecue chicken, cut into bite-size pieces
1 large tomato, diced
1/3 cup (10 g) chopped fresh flat-leaf parsley
3/4 cup (90 g) shredded Cheddar

1. Bring a large pan of salted water to the boil and cook the macaroni according to the manufacturer's instructions, adding the frozen peas to the pan just before the macaroni finishes cooking. Drain well.
2. Meanwhile, put the ricotta cheese, Parmesan and oil in a pan. Mix to combine and place over a medium-low heat. Season with salt and black pepper. Add the chicken, tomato and parsley. Heat through until hot, then keep warm over a low heat. Preheat the grill.
3. Place the macaroni and peas in a shallow ovenproof dish about 20 x 30 cm. Add the chicken mixture and toss to combine. Sprinkle the Cheddar over the surface.
4. Place under the grill and cook until the cheese melts and browns. Serve with some vegetables.

NUTRITION PER SERVE *Protein 30 g; Fat 25 g; Carbohydrate 35 g; Dietary Fibre 3.5 g; Cholesterol 100 mg; 2065 kJ (495 cal)*

Two-minute noodle and vegetable omelette (top) with Cheesy chicken macaroni

Fettucine with ham and corn

*Ready to eat in
20 minutes
Serves 4*

400 g fettucine
2 x 310 g cans
creamed corn
1 cup (125 ml) cream
80 g ham, cut into
strips
2 tablespoons finely
chopped fresh parsley

1. Fill a large pan with salted water and bring to the boil. Add the fettucine, stir well to separate the strands and cook according to the manufacturer's instructions. Drain well.
2. Meanwhile, heat the creamed corn and cream in another pan until boiling, then reduce the heat and add the ham. Simmer for 3 minutes and season to taste with salt and freshly ground black pepper.
3. Divide the fettucine among four serving plates and pour over the ham and corn sauce. Toss gently, then scatter with the parsley and serve.

NUTRITION PER SERVE
*Protein 15 g; Fat 15 g;
Carbohydrate 95 g; Dietary
Fibre 10 g; Cholesterol
40 mg; 2475 kJ (590 cal)*

Vegetable stir-fry

*Ready to eat in
30 minutes
Serves 4*

2 tablespoons
peanut oil
250 g firm tofu, cut
into cubes
2 cloves garlic, crushed
1 teaspoon grated
fresh ginger
1 zucchini, halved
lengthways and sliced
1 carrot, halved
lengthways and sliced
1 small red capsicum,
cut into short
thin strips
150 g small broccoli
florets
2 tablespoons teriyaki
marinade sauce
1/4 cup (60 ml) orange
juice
1 tablespoon honey
1 tablespoon sesame
seeds

1. Heat the wok until very hot, then add 1 tablespoon of the peanut oil and swirl to coat the sides. Fry the tofu in batches until golden, adding more oil if necessary. Remove from the pan and drain on paper towels.
2. Add the remaining oil to the wok and stir-fry the garlic and ginger for 1 minute.

Add the zucchini, carrot, capsicum and broccoli and stir-fry over a high heat for 3–4 minutes.
3. Return the tofu to the wok with the teriyaki marinade sauce, orange juice and honey. Toss to coat in the sauce and stir-fry for 2–3 minutes. Sprinkle with sesame seeds and serve with some steamed rice or noodles.

NUTRITION PER SERVE
*Protein 7 g; Fat 15 g;
Carbohydrate 10 g; Dietary
Fibre 3.5 g; Cholesterol
0 mg; 645 kJ (155 cal)*

*Fettucine with ham and corn (top) with
Vegetable stir-fry*

PIZZAS

Beef and cherry tomato pizzas

Add oil to a frying pan and cook 2 steaks sliced into strips with 2 crushed cloves of garlic until browned. Spread 4 small pizza bases with a thin layer of tomato paste mixed with a teaspoon of mixed herbs. Sprinkle with grated cheese and top with half a red onion cut in wedges, the beef and a few halved cherry tomatoes. Bake for 10 minutes in a hot 220°C (425°F/ Gas 7) oven until the bases are golden and crisp. Sprinkle with shredded basil.

Mexican pizza

Fry a chopped onion and 2 crushed cloves of garlic in a little oil until soft. Add 400 g lean minced beef and fry, breaking up any lumps witrh a wooden spoon, until well browned. Add some taco seasoning and half a can of refried beans and stir to combine. Spread 2 large pizza bases with a little taco sauce, top with the mince and sprinkle with grated mozarella. Bake for 10–15 minutes in a hot 220°C (425°F/ Gas 7) oven, or until the bases are golden and crisp. Serve topped with guacamole and sour cream.

Stir-fry vegetable pizza

In a wok or large, heavy-based frying pan, stir-fry a packet of frozen chow-mein vegetable mix with 2 crushed cloves of garlic and a good splash of oyster sauce over high heat until the vegetables are just tender and cooked through and almost all the sauce has evaporated off. Spread a large pizza base with a thin layer of tomato paste and sprinkle over a layer of grated mozarella. Top with the stir-fried vegetables and a sprinkling of sesame seeds.

Bake for about 10 minutes in a hot 220°C (425°F/Gas 7) oven, or until the base is golden and crisp.

Chicken tikka masala pizza

Add some oil to a frying pan and cook 250 g chicken strips until golden brown and cooked through. Add 2 teaspoons of tikka masala paste and cook for 1 minute, or until the chicken is coated in the paste. Transfer to a bowl and stir in 4 tablespoons thick plain yoghurt. Spread a large pizza base with a layer of mango chutney. Top with the chicken strips and bake in a hot 220°C (425°F/Gas 7) oven for 10–15 minutes, or until the base is golden and crisp. Sprinkle over some chopped fresh coriander and drizzle with extra yoghurt.

Ham and pineapple pizza

Spread 2 large Lebanese breads evenly with a thin layer of tomato paste. Top the tomato paste with a handful of thin ham strips and a few pieces of chopped fresh or well-drained canned pineapple. Sprinkle with a generous layer of grated mozzarella cheese and bake for about 10 minutes in a hot 220°C (425°F/ Gas 7) oven, or until the bases are golden and crisp.

From left to right: Beef and cherry tomato; Mexican; Stir-fry vegetable; Chicken tikka masala; Ham and pineapple

Chicken burritos

Ready to eat in 30 minutes
Makes 8

375 g packet flour
   tortillas
1 barbecued chicken
325 g jar mild salsa
2 large tomatoes,
   sliced
3 cups (135 g) shredded
   lettuce
1 Lebanese cucumber,
   sliced
2 cups (250 g) grated
   Cheddar

1. Preheat the oven
to moderate 180°C
(350°F/Gas 4). Wrap
the flour tortillas
in foil and place on a
baking tray. Warm in
the oven for about
10 minutes.
2. Meanwhile skin,
bone and shred the
barbecued chicken.
Place the chicken in
a pan with the jar of
salsa and stir together
until heated through.
Arrange some of the
shredded chicken
and the sauce in the
middle of each of the
warm tortillas.
3. Pile the tomato,
lettuce, cucumber and
cheese on top of the
chicken in the tortillas.
Roll up and serve.

NUTRITION PER BURRITO
*Protein 10 g; Fat 15 g;
Carbohydrate 3.5 g; Dietary
Fibre 1.5 g; Cholesterol
30 mg; 806 kJ (185 cal)*

Porcupine balls with pasta

Ready to eat in 30 minutes.
Serves 4

250 g beef mince
1/2 onion, chopped
2 cloves garlic, crushed
1/2 carrot, grated
1 teaspoon dried mixed
   herbs
1/2 cup (110 g)
   short-grain rice
150 g pasta wheels,
   twirls or any variety
   your kids like
500 g can tomato
   soup
1/2 cup (125 ml) milk
1 tablespoon chopped
   fresh parsley
3 tablespoons grated
   Parmesan, for serving

1. Combine the beef
mince, onion, garlic,
carrot, mixed herbs,
rice and some salt and
freshly ground black
pepper in a large bowl.
Mix well with your
hands and roll into
16 equal-sized balls.
2. Heat the tomato
soup, milk and
1 1/2 cups (375 ml)
water together in a pan.

Once the mixture
comes to the boil,
reduce the heat and
add the meatballs.
3. Cook the meatballs
for about 20 minutes,
stirring occasionally,
until the rice and meat
are cooked through.
When the meatballs
have finished cooking,
stir in the parsley.
4. Meanwhile, fill a
large pan with salted
water and bring to
the boil. Add the pasta
and cook according to
the manufacturer's
instructions. Drain well.
5. Divide the pasta
among four plates and
place the porcupine
balls and tomato sauce
on top. Serve with
the Parmesan.

NUTRITION PER SERVE
*Protein 25 g; Fat 10 g;
Carbohydrate 65 g; Dietary
Fibre 6 g; Cholesterol
50 mg; 1925 kJ (460 cal)*

Note: You can cook
this dish in the
microwave if you wish.
Place in a microwave-
proof dish and cook on
Medium-High for
10 minutes, or until
the rice and meat are
cooked through. The
meatballs can also be
made in advance and
frozen for up to
3 months if you wish.
Place in a plastic
container and seal well.
Defrost before using.

*Chicken burritos (top) with
Porcupine balls with pasta*

Lamb cutlets with apple, walnut and carrot salad

Ready to eat in
20 minutes
Serves 4

500 g floury potatoes,
peeled and cubed
8 lamb cutlets,
well trimmed
1 tablespoon light
olive oil
2–3 tablespoons
mint jelly
3 tablespoons milk
40 g butter

Apple, walnut and
carrot salad
1¹/2 carrots, coarsely
grated
1 red apple, unpeeled
and coarsely grated
1 stick celery, finely
sliced
¹/4 cup (30 g) walnut
pieces
2 teaspoons finely
chopped fresh mint
3 tablespoons coleslaw
dressing

1. Place the potato in a large pan of salted water, bring to the boil and cook for 8 minutes, or until tender. Preheat the grill to medium hot.
2. Brush the lamb cutlets on both sides with the olive oil, then spread a thin coating of mint jelly over them. Place under the hot grill and cook for 2–3 minutes each side until browned and cooked through.
3. To make the apple, walnut and carrot salad, place the carrot, apple, celery, walnuts, mint and coleslaw dressing in a large bowl and mix together well.
4. Drain the potatoes, then mash with milk and butter. Season with salt and black pepper.
5. Spoon a pile of mashed potato onto each of four plates. Arrange two cutlets on top and serve with the salad.

NUTRITION PER SERVE
Protein 18 g; Fat 25 g;
Carbohydrate 25 g; Dietary
Fibre 4 g; Cholesterol
75 mg; 1710 kJ (410 cal)

Honey sesame meatballs

Ready to eat in
30 minutes
Makes 24 meatballs

500 g lean beef mince
2 tablespoons soy sauce
1 egg, lightly beaten
¹/4 cup (25 g) dry
breadcrumbs
1 tablespoon honey
¹/2 cup (80 g) sesame
seeds
2 tablespoons oil

1. In a bowl, combine the mince, soy, egg, breadcrumbs and honey. Using wet hands, roll tablespoonfuls of the mince mixture into balls and set aside on a plate.
2. Place the sesame seeds on a plate and roll the balls in them, pressing on firmly. Heat the oil in a large non-stick frying pan and cook the meatballs in batches over medium heat, turning carefully, until golden and cooked. Drain on paper towels and serve as snacks on cocktail sticks or with rice.

NUTRITION PER MEATBALL
Protein 5.5 g; Fat 6 g;
Carbohydrate 2 g; Dietary
Fibre 0.5 g; Cholesterol
20 mg; 340 kJ (80 cal)

Note: Don't give cocktail sticks to small children.

Lamb cutlets with apple, walnut and carrot salad
(top) with Honey sesame meatballs

Herb and Parmesan-crusted fish with quick guacamole

Ready to eat in
  25 minutes
Serves 4

1/4 cup (30 g) plain
  flour, to coat
2 x 250 g skinless
  fish fillets, cut into
  2 pieces each (see
  Note)
3 tablespoons dried
  breadcrumbs
2 tablespoons grated
  Parmesan
1 tablespoon chopped
  fresh parsley
2 teaspoons chopped
  fresh dill
1 tablespoon flaked
  almonds, roughly
  chopped
1 egg
1 tablespoon milk
2 tablespoons oil

Quick guacamole
200 g tub guacamole
  dip
1 small ripe tomato,
  deseeded and finely
  chopped
1/2 onion, finely
  chopped

1. Place the flour in a shallow dish and coat the fish evenly. Combine the breadcrumbs, Parmesan, parsley, dill and almonds in a shallow dish. Whisk together the egg and milk in another shallow dish. Dip the fish into the combined egg and milk, then coat the fish with the breadcrumb mixture, ensuring the crumbs are pressed down firmly onto the fish. Leave the fish to stand while you make the guacamole.
2. To make the guacamole, combine the dip, tomato and onion in a small bowl.
3. Heat the oil in a frying pan until hot. Cook the fish over medium heat for about 3 minutes each side, or until golden brown and cooked through.
4. Drain the fish on paper towels and serve with guacamole on top. Accompany with salad and oven-baked chips.

NUTRITION PER SERVE
Protein 35 g; Fat 30 g;
Carbohydrate 10 g; Dietary
Fibre 2 g; Cholesterol
200 mg; 1900 kJ (455 cal)

Note: Use a fish that has few or no bones. A good variety is fillet of ling or blue-eyed cod, which have only a few easily removed bones. Alternatively, use fish cutlets.

Vegetable and macaroni soup

Ready to eat in
  30 minutes
Serves 4–6

1 tablespoon oil
1 onion, cut into
  1 cm cubes
1 large carrot, cut into
  1 cm cubes
1 large zucchini, cut
  into 1 cm cubes
1 litre chicken stock
1/2 cup (80 g) macaroni
1 tablespoon tomato
  paste
300 g can kidney
  beans, drained

1. Heat the oil in a large pan, add the vegetables and cook for 5 minutes, or until soft. Meanwhile, bring the stock to the boil. Add the stock to the vegetables and cover with a lid to quickly bring to the boil. When boiling, uncover the pan and cook for about 8 minutes, or until the vegetables are tender.
2. Add the macaroni and tomato paste. Return to the boil and cook for 8 minutes, or until the pasta is tender. Add the beans, salt and pepper and stir until hot.

NUTRITION PER SERVE (6)
Protein 5.5 g; Fat 3.5 g;
Carbohydrate 18 g; Dietary
Fibre 5 g; Cholesterol
0 mg; 545 kJ (130 cal)

Herb and Parmesan-crusted fish with quick guacamole (top) and Vegetable and macaroni soup

Sausage and pasta bake

*Ready to eat in
  30 minutes*
Serves 6

2^1/2 cups (225 g)
  penne pasta
10 thin sausages
*1 small onion,
  chopped*
2 carrots, diced
2 zucchini, diced
225 g can baked beans
*425 g can crushed
  tomatoes*
*1 cup (125 g) grated
  Cheddar*
^{1}/2 *cup (125 g) sour
  cream*
*2 tablespoons dry
  breadcrumbs*

1. Bring a large pan of
salted water to the boil
and cook the pasta
according to the
manufacturer's
instructions. Drain well.
2. Meanwhile, in a
large frying pan,
cook the sausages for
2–3 minutes, or until
cooked through.
Remove from the pan
and slice into pieces.
3. Add the onion,
carrot and zucchini to
the pan. Cook over a
medium-high heat for
2–3 minutes, or until
the onion has softened.
Add the baked beans
and tomatoes, bring to
the boil, then remove
from the heat.

4. Preheat the grill.
Mix together the
vegetable mixture,
sliced sausages, half
the Cheddar, the sour
cream and the cooked
penne pasta. Spoon
into a 2.5 litre
ovenproof dish.
5. Sprinkle the
remaining Cheddar
and breadcrumbs over
the top and grill until
golden brown.

NUTRITION PER SERVE
*Protein 15 g; Fat 25 g;
Carbohydrate 40 g; Dietary
Fibre 6 g; Cholesterol
55 mg; 1815 kJ (435 cal)*

Pasta with chickpeas

*Ready to eat in
  30 minutes*
Serves 6

*3 cups (270 g) spiral
  pasta*
1 tablespoon oil
*1 large onion,
  chopped*
2 cloves garlic, crushed
*2 x 425 g cans crushed
  tomatoes*
*1 tablespoon tomato
  paste*
*425 g can chickpeas,
  drained*
*1 teaspoon dried Italian
  herbs*
2 teaspoons sugar
*1 cup (125 g) finely
  grated cheese*

1. Bring a large pan
of salted water to the
boil and cook the
pasta according to
the manufacturer's
instructions. Drain well.
2. Meanwhile, heat the
oil in a large pan, add
the onion and cook for
2–3 minutes, or until
soft. Add the garlic and
cook for 1 minute. Add
the tomatoes, tomato
paste, chickpeas, Italian
herbs and sugar. Bring
to the boil, reduce the
heat and simmer for
10 minutes. Preheat
the grill.
3. Return the pasta to
the pan, then add the
tomato mixture and stir
to combine.
4. Transfer the mixture
to a large shallow
baking dish or six
individual baking
dishes, and sprinkle
with the cheese. Cook
under the grill until the
cheese is just melted
and bubbling. Serve
with some steamed
green vegetables.

NUTRITION PER SERVE
*Protein 15 g; Fat 10 g;
Carbohydrate 45 g; Dietary
Fibre 7.5 g; Cholesterol
20 mg; 1495 kJ (355 cal)*

Note: Borlotti or
butter beans can be
substituted for
chickpeas if preferred.

*Sausage and pasta bake (top)
and Pasta with chickpeas*

Sweet treats

Dessert is the best part of a meal for most kids. If you don't want to spend hours in the kitchen, try one of these quick ideas.

Little jellies

*Ready to eat in
30 minutes
Serves 6*

2^1/2 *cups (600 ml)
freshly squeezed
orange juice*
6 teaspoons gelatine
2 bananas
12 strawberries
yoghurt, to serve
*mint sprigs, to garnish,
optional*

1. Pour ^{1}/2 cup of the orange juice into a small heatproof bowl, sprinkle the gelatine in an even layer over the surface and leave to go spongy.
2. Place 1 cup of the orange juice in a small pan and bring to the boil. Turn off the heat and add the gelatine mixture, then stir until thoroughly dissolved.
3. Slice the bananas and strawberries and divide among six ^{1}/2 cup (125 ml) ramekins or jelly dishes. Pour in the jelly (don't worry if the fruit floats). Put the jellies in the freezer for about 20 minutes, or until set.
4. Serve the jellies with a dollop of yoghurt and a mint sprig.

NUTRITION PER SERVE
*Protein 4 g; Fat 0 g;
Carbohydrate 20 g; Dietary
Fibre 1.5 g; Cholesterol
0 mg; 440 kJ (105 cal)*

Note: These jellies do not turn out of the moulds very well, so set them in glasses or jelly dishes. Do not leave in the freezer if you aren't serving them straight away. Move to the refrigerator as soon as they are set.

Little jellies

Rocky road

*Ready to eat in
30 minutes
Serves 8*

375 g milk chocolate,
  chopped
30 g Copha (white
  vegetable shortening),
  chopped
200 g mini pink
  and white
  marshmallows
$1/3$ cup (30 g)
  desiccated coconut
$1/3$ cup (70 g) glacé
  cherries, halved
$1/3$ cup (45 g)
  macadamia pieces

1. Lightly grease a
19 cm square cake tin.
Line the base and sides
with non-stick baking
paper, leaving a little
hanging over each side
so you can lift the rocky
road out of the tin.
2. Combine the
chocolate and Copha in
a heatproof bowl. Bring
a pan of water to the
boil, then remove the
pan from the heat. Sit
the bowl over the pan,
making sure the bottom
of the bowl is not
sitting in the water.
Stir the chocolate
occasionally until it has
melted. (Alternatively,
microwave on High for
1 minute, stirring twice

during cooking.)
3. Combine the
chocolate and the
remaining ingredients
in a bowl, spread over
the base of the
prepared tin and
smooth the surface.
Freeze the rocky road
for 15–20 minutes, or
until set. Cut into
pieces to serve.

NUTRITION PER SERVE
*Protein 4 g; Fat 25 g;
Carbohydrate 35 g; Dietary
Fibre 1 g; Cholesterol
8.5 mg; 1550 kJ (352 cal)*

Chocolate-coated bananas

*Ready to eat in
30 minutes
Serves 4*

2 bananas
4 paddle pop sticks or
  a pair of disposable
  chopsticks
$1/3$ cup (80 ml)
  Chocolate Ice Magic
2 tablespoons sprinkles,
  hundreds and
  thousands or nuts

1. Peel the bananas and
cut each one in half
lengthways. Push the
paddle pop sticks
gently into the bananas
to make a handle.
(If you're using
chopsticks, break them
in half first.)

2. Warm the Chocolate
Ice Magic in a pan or
microwave according
to the manufacturer's
instructions, then pour
the chocolate into a tall
narrow glass. Twirl the
bananas in the
chocolate and place on
a baking tray lined with
baking paper. (You will
find that you have
excess chocolate, but
you need enough so
you can twirl the
bananas around in the
chocolate and coat
them evenly.)
3. If you want the
bananas to have a
thicker coat of
chocolate, allow them
to set in the freezer for
5 minutes, then recoat
them in the Chocolate
Ice Magic.
4. Tip the sprinkles
or hundreds and
thousands on to
separate plates for each
colour and roll the
bananas in them while
the coating is still wet.
5. Put the bananas on
a plate and place in the
freezer for 10 minutes
to set.

NUTRITION PER SERVE
*Protein 1 g; Fat 0 g;
Carbohydrate 25 g; Dietary
Fibre 1.5 g; Cholesterol
0 mg; 415 kJ (100 cal)*

Note: The bananas can
be made and left in the
freezer until needed if
you wish.

*Rocky road (top) with
Chocolate-coated bananas*

Fresh fruity slushies

*Ready to eat in
  30 minutes
Makes 4*

*250 g fresh
  strawberries,
  trimmed and
  washed
1 banana, sliced
1/3 cup (80 ml) milk
200 g tub flavoured
  yoghurt (any flavour
  you like)
plastic cups or ice-
  block moulds
  (available from
  some supermarkets)*

1. Place the
strawberries, banana,
milk and yoghurt in a
food processor or
blender, and process
until slightly chunky or
smooth, depending on
the texture you prefer.
2. Pour the mixture
into the plastic cups or
ice-block moulds.
3. Place in the freezer
for about 25 minutes,
then stir the frozen
edges into the centre
of the slushies and
serve immediately.

NUTRITION PER SLUSHY
*Protein 5 g; Fat 3 g;
Carbohydrate 15 g; Dietary
Fibre 2 g; Cholesterol
8.5 mg; 435 kJ (105 cal)*

Note: If you want, you
can make these into
solid ice pops by
freezing them until

semi-frozen, then
pushing paddle pop
sticks into them.
Return to the freezer
and freeze until solid.
When you are ready
to eat them, remove the
frozen slushies from
freezer, then take them
out of the moulds.

Frûche and fruit salad

*Ready to eat in
  10 minutes
Serves 4*

*1/2 small pineapple,
  peeled, cored and
  cut into cubes or
  1 small can of
  pineapple pieces.
1 red apple, cored
  and chopped
  into cubes
1 banana, peeled
  and sliced
1 cup (180 g) red
  grapes, pips
  removed or 1 cup
  (200 g) stoneless
  cherries
2 x 200 g tubs vanilla
  or flavoured Frûche
  (fromage frais)*

1. Toss all the fruit
together in large bowl,
then divide about half
the fruit evenly into
four 1 cup (250 ml)
capacity glass tumblers

or dishes.
2. Stir the Frûche gently
to soften. Top with half
the Frûche, then place
the remaining fruit on
top to make a third
layer. Finish with a
fourth layer of the
remaining Frûche.

NUTRITION PER SERVE
*Protein 2 g; Fat 4 g;
Carbohydrate 25 g; Dietary
Fibre 3 g; Cholesterol
0 mg; 885 kJ (200 cal)*

Note: Use any fruit in
season for this recipe.
Try oranges, pears and
stone fruits. You can
also use yoghurt
instead of Frûche if
you prefer.

---

*Fresh fruity slushies (top)
with Frûche and fruit salad*

Poached fruit with waffles and honey yoghurt

*Ready to eat in
15 minutes
Serves 4*

*1/4 cup (90 g) honey
2 large green apples,
  peeled, cored and
  quartered
2 large firm ripe pears,
  peeled, cored and
  quartered
8 waffles
2 x 200 g tubs
  honey-flavoured
  yoghurt*

1. Place the honey and 1 cup (250 ml) water in a large pan and bring to the boil.
2. Cut the apple and pear quarters in half lengthways. Add the fruit to the honey syrup. Cover and cook over a low heat for 8 minutes, stirring occasionally, until the fruit is tender.
3. To serve, warm the waffles in the oven or microwave according to the manufacturer's instructions.
4. Place one or two waffles on each plate. Arrange some of the apple and pear on the waffles, then pour over the cooking syrup. Top with a dollop of honey-flavoured yoghurt and serve immediately.

NUTRITION PER SERVE
*Protein 5 g; Fat 4.5 g;
Carbohydrate 45 g; Dietary
Fibre 2.5 g; Cholesterol
15 mg; 1324 kJ (300 cal)*

Fruity barbecue kebabs

*Ready to eat in
20 minutes
Makes 8 kebabs*

*8 bamboo skewers
  (see Note)
1 kiwi fruit
1/2 small pineapple
2 bananas
1 green apple
8 strawberries
1/4 cup (90 g) honey
1/4 cup (60 ml) orange
  juice*

1. Soak the bamboo skewers in water while you prepare the fruit.
2. Peel and cut the kiwi fruit into eight even-sized pieces. Remove the skin and core from the pineapple, and cut into 3 cm pieces. Cut the bananas into 8 even-sized pieces. Peel and core the apple and cut into eight even-sized pieces. Remove the hulls from the strawberries.
3. Thread one piece of each fruit onto the bamboo skewers in a pretty pattern.
4. Preheat a barbecue hot plate or an oven grill. Combine the honey and orange juice in a small bowl.
5. Brush the honey and juice over the fruit and cook for about 6 minutes, turning halfway through cooking. Take care not to overcook or the fruit will fall off the skewers. Brush with the honey and juice mixture during the cooking.
6. Serve the fruit skewers with a little of the honey and juice mixture drizzled over. Delicious with yoghurt or ice cream.

NUTRITION PER KEBAB
*Protein 1.5 g; Fat 0 g;
Carbohydrate 25 g; Dietary
Fibre 2.5 g; Cholesterol
0 mg; 465 kJ (110 cal)*

Note: It is important to soak the skewers first or they will burn on the barbecue. You can use short or long skewers for this recipe.
You can also use any fruit on the skewers, provided it is not too soft, or it may fall off as it cooks. Remove the fruit from the skewers if you are serving these fruity kebabs to very young children.

*Poached fruit with waffles and honey yoghurt
(top) with Fruity barbecue kebabs*

DRINKS

Strawberry soy thickshake

For each person, place half a glass of vanilla-flavoured soy milk, a scoop of vanilla or strawberry tofu ice cream, a handful of strawberries and a tablespoon of honey in a blender. Blend until smooth and thick, then pour into tall glasses to serve.

Fruit crush

For each person, place about 6 ice cubes in a plastic bag and crush them with a meat mallet or rolling pin. Place the crushed ice in a blender with $1/4$ glass of pineapple juice and $1/2$ glass of fresh orange and mango juice. Blend until combined, then pour into tall glasses to serve.

Iced banana smoothie

For each person, put a banana, $3/4$ glass of milk, a scoop of vanilla ice cream, and 2 teaspoons of honey in a blender. Blend until smooth, then pour into glasses and dust with a little ground cinnamon.

Cola ice cream soda

For each person, fill a tall glass up to halfway full with cola, then add a scoop of vanilla ice cream. The ice cream will make the cola foam up, so serve immediately. For a variation, you could try lemonade instead of cola.

Fruity punch

Combine 10 chopped strawberries, $1/2$ peeled and chopped pineapple, 2 peeled and segmented oranges and 2 peeled and chopped kiwi fruit in a large punch bowl (you can change the fruit depending on the season). Add 2 glasses of pineapple juice, 2 glasses of dry ginger ale and 2 glasses of lemonade and stir gently to combine. Stir in 2 tablespoons chopped fresh mint leaves and ladle into 6–8 glasses to serve.

Warm chocolate marshmallow drink

For each person, put a mug full of milk in a pan. Add 1 tablespoon drinking chocolate per mug and stir over a low heat until dissolved. When dissolved, turn up the heat until the chocolate is hot, then pour back into the mug. Top each with a spoonful of whipped cream, marshmallows and drinking chocolate.

From left to right: Strawberry soy thickshake; Fruit crush; Iced banana smoothie; Cola ice cream soda; Fruity punch; Warm chocolate marshmallow drink

Index